To the Daniel's

Passover 2008

from the NEMBER/REID Family

"LET MY PEOPLE GO, THAT THEY MAY SERVE ME."

(EXODUS 9:1)

מעשה

בר׳ אליעזר ור׳ יהושע ור׳ אלעזר

בן עזריה ור׳ עקיבא ור׳ טרפון שה
יו מסובין בבני ברק והיו מספרים
ביציאת מצרים כל אותו הלילה
עד שבאו תלמידהם ואמר
ו להם רבותינו הגיע זמן קריאת
שמע של שחרית:

אמר ר׳ אלעזר בן עזרי
הרי אני כבן
שבעים שנה
ולא זכיתי שתאמר יציאת מצ
בלילות עד שדרשה בן זומ

PASSOVER SPLENDOR

CHERISHED OBJECTS FOR THE SEDER TABLE

Barbara Rush

A FAIR STREET BOOK

Stewart Tabori & Chang
New York

Published in 2004 by
Stewart, Tabori & Chang
A Company of La Martinière Groupe
115 West 18th Street
New York, NY 10011

Export sales to all countries except Canada, France, and French-speaking Switzerland:
Thames and Hudson Ltd.
181A High Holborn
London WC1V 7QX
England

Canadian Distribution:
Canadian Manda Group
One Atlantic Avenue, Suite 105
Toronto, Ontario M6K 3E7
Canada

Library of Congress Cataloging-in-Publication Data

Rush, Barbara.
    Splendor of Passover : festival of freedom / Barbara Rush.-- 1st ed.
       p. cm.
    "A Fair Street book."
    ISBN 1-58479-399-6
    1. Passover. I. Title.

BM695.P3R89 2005
296.4'37--dc22
                                    2004016065
ISBN: 1-58479-399-6

Produced by Fair Street Productions, New York City
Directors: Deborah Bull, Susan Wechsler

Designer: Jon Glick
Photo Researcher: Shaie Dively/Photosearch, Inc.
Copyeditor: Lesley Krauss

The text of this book was composed in Perpetua and Twentieth Century.

Printed in China

10 9 8 7 6 5 4 3 2 1

First Printing

CONTENTS

The Exodus Story   6

Introduction   9

Order of the Seder   14

The Haggadah: Book of Freedom   17

Seder Plates   39

Cups   61

Textiles   77

Blessings for the Seder   92

Songs   94

Acknowledgments   96

The Exodus Story

THE LIBERATION OF THE ISRAELITES from bondage and their subsequent exodus from Egypt probably took place about three thousand years ago, sometime between 1250 and 1450 B.C.E. Conflicting data from scholars of archaeology, history, genealogy, and the Bible make pinpointing the exact date (and the people involved) a difficult task. According to the Book of Exodus, and later biblical/post-biblical works, this is the story:

About 1700 B.C.E. there was a famine in the land of the Israelites, and many went south to Egypt to find food. After generations of peace, a new ruler—believed by some to be Rameses II—feared that the six hundred thousand–strong Hebrew men might rise against him. Determined to curb their numbers, he forced them to toil both in the fields and the cities, and ordered their newborn sons to be killed.

When the people could no longer endure their slavery, God chose Moses and his brother, Aaron, to plead with Pharoah to free the Israelites to serve their God in the wilderness. But Pharoah refused, so God inflicted nine terrible plagues—one at a time—upon the land of the Egyptians: blood in the river, frogs, lice, wild beasts, disease of cattle, boils, hail, locusts, and thick darkness. Since Pharaoh only relented until each plague was lifted, God sent the tenth—and most terrible—plague upon Egypt: death to the firstborn in every home. God commanded the Israelites to splash the blood of a sacrificed lamb upon their doorposts, so the Angel of Death would know to "pass over" them. That night, as death struck every Egyptian home, the Israelites (at God's command) quickly ate their meals of roast meat, bitter herbs, and bread that was left unleavened, since it was baked in haste. They fled quickly to the shores of the sea, but Pharaoh sent his warriors in pursuit.

As the biblical story relates, God caused the waters to part, and the Israelites crossed over safely on dry ground. Then, as the soldiers of Pharoah entered the sea, God caused the waters to return, and the soldiers drowned. Joyfully, Moses sang songs of praise and thanks to God, and Miriam, his sister, led the women in a dance of freedom.

And so, a little more than four hundred years after first entering Egypt, the Israelites began their long journey back to Canaan.

זה הסדר הקערה של פסח לכי

ג מצות

כתר חכמה בינה

כהן לוי ישראל

חסד גבורה

זרוע

נצה חרוסת כרפס

ביצה הוד מלכות

יהקערה

לרשות הצ כרפס יחץ

מניד רחצה מוציא מצה מרור

כורך שלחן עורך

צפון ברך הלל נרצה

Introduction

PASSOVER, THROUGHOUT CENTURIES, has been and still is the most widely celebrated home holiday, observed and revered by Jews everywhere. In the darkest of times and direst of circumstances—in concentration camps, in hiding during wars, and while escaping to new lands—Jews have endeavored to observe and participate in this festival of freedom. Passover, called *Pesach* in Hebrew, celebrates the deliverance by God more than three thousand years ago of the children of Israel from bondage in Egypt. This powerful historical memory, vividly described in the Book of Exodus, is also relevant for celebrations today—and for those in the future: "Remember this day, in which ye came out from Egypt, out of the house of bondage." "Ye shall keep it a feast by an ordinance forever." (Exodus 13:3 and 12:14)

Passover has several names: sometimes called the Festival of Spring, it coincides with the anniversary of the exodus, on the fifteenth of the Hebrew month, Nisan, that usually falls in April; many customs, such as the eating of greens, are symbolic of the season. Passover's other names—the Festival of Unleavened Bread and the Festival of the Paschal Offering—are rooted in early, pre-Israelite celebrations. Such holidays, occurring during the season of harvest and lambing, served as a release from the harshness of winter. In biblical times, as the exodus became a central idea in Jewish life, the Passover celebration focused on the first Passover meal, as commanded by God to the children of Israel before they hurriedly left Egypt. The Torah relates: "And they shall eat the flesh in that night, roast with fire, and unleavened bread with bitter herbs...." (Exodus 12:8) During the time of the Second Temple (destroyed in 70 C.E.), Jews from the rest of the country—and from Rome, Egypt, Syria, Babylonia, and elsewhere—flocked to Jerusalem for the sacrifice of lambs; the meat was then eaten at home with matzah—the flat wafer baked by the children of Israel in haste—and with bitter herbs. Throughout later centuries and until today, the lamb, matzah, and bitter herbs have been and are integral parts of the Passover table.

Haggadah Shel Pesach, Baghdad, 1883, Moshe Yosef Avraham
The Gross Family Collection, Tel Aviv

The name by which Passover is best known is the Season of Our Freedom. The story of this freedom—the story of the exodus—is told and taught on Passover eve at a festive meal called the seder, which is so special, so different, and so magical that it is thought of as "the meal of all meals." The telling of the story by parents to children is mandated, not once but four times, in the Torah: Exodus 12:26, 13:3, 13:8; Deuteronomy 6:20.

The word "seder" in Hebrew means order or arrangement, and the seder indeed follows a certain order. Although Jews from both Ashkenazi and Sephardi backgrounds enjoy the same festive meal, the term "seder" is used mostly by Jews of Ashkenazi tradition. But despite variations in custom, the seder is virtually the same in every Jewish home. Family and friends come together to celebrate; it is also traditional to invite strangers and non-Jews to join as guests. The Passover celebration, oriented toward the family, is especially geared toward children. Thus, during the seder, a child asks four questions, the answers to which launch the telling of the entire story; later in the meal, children find and ransom a special piece of matzah (the *afikoman*). And, in some haggadahs (books that establish the order of the seder), there are special sections designed for children.

The seder, as a ceremony of remembrance, took hold in the first century C.E., after the destruction, by Rome, of the Holy Temple. Passover then moved from the Temple to the home. The basis of celebration—observing the festival, telling the story, sacrificing the Paschal lamb, eating the bitter herbs, eating only unleavened bread, and even ridding the home of leaven—are of divine command. But it was later rabbinic interpretation that explained, embellished, and extended biblical injunctions, and it is these details of the seder ritual that Jews now perform. Most are set forth in the tractate Pesahim of the Mishnah (the early part of the Talmud, completed by 200 C.E.). Such laws were further extended in tractates of the same name in later parts of the two Talmuds (redacted in Israel and Babylonia and concluded by 500 C.E.). These include the precise ritual of removing leaven from the home (before the seder), the order of the seder meal, the rules of the Paschal offering, the regulations for making matzah, the partaking of four cups of wine, the asking of questions by the son and the response of the father, and more. Many practices (e.g., placing a burnt egg and lamb shank bone on the table) are in remembrance of the Temple or relate to rituals of Temple times; others—such as reclining while eating—bear the influence of surrounding Greco-Roman culture, where leaning while eating was a sign of being free. Another rabbinic ritual is the obligation of mentioning the *Pesach* (the Paschal offering) at the seder meal; this refers to God's commandment to the children of Israel to splash blood of a slain lamb on their doorposts. God promised, "I will go through the land of Egypt in that (last) night, and will smite all the first born in the land of Egypt...and the blood shall be to you for a token upon your houses, and when I see the blood, I will pass over you...." (Exodus 12:12, 13) The name of the festival, *Pesach*, which in Hebrew means to skip or pass over, comes from this passage.

At this time and later, Midrash (stories told by the rabbis to interpret a biblical story) also contributed to Passover lore. So too did the writings of Jewish historians in Roman times. And, during hundreds of years that followed, the seder was further strengthened by the greatest commentators on and the greatest compilers of Jewish law: Rashi in the eleventh century, Maimonides in the twelfth, Joseph Caro in the sixteenth, as well as many others. In addition, during those hundreds of years and up until the present, Passover rituals have been and continue to be shaped by local custom and family tradition. Bitter herbs, for example, may be romaine lettuce as eaten by Jews of Yemen, horseradish as used in Eastern Europe, or artichokes as found in Gibraltar.

Matzah Perforator Wheel, Southern Germany, 19th Century
The Israel Museum, Jerusalem

The Passover seder, this meal of deliverance, strives to celebrate all types of freedoms: political, national, spiritual, and religious. And for every participant, each part of the seder is a step towards his or her own personal liberation. The first part of the seder is largely a recitation of the biblical story, yet this special meal does more than tell a story of the past. Each year, through its rituals and readings, the seder expands the story of the Israelites' liberation, thus acting as a continuum to the present. The seder stimulates every participant to act towards bringing freedom to others: to the poor, the needy, the oppressed, and the enslaved. Each participant may ask, "As God helped the children of Israel 'with an outstretched arm,' how can I reach out to others?"

The second half of the seder looks to the future. The biblical story of redemption expands to include peace and freedom for all people, upon the coming of the Messiah. It is believed that this event will be heralded by Elijah the Prophet, God's messenger, as he enters Jerusalem. In this way, the Passover celebration not only celebrates a past liberation but also gives hope for both the present and the future.

Passover may be a seven- or eight-day celebration. "Seven days thou shall eat unleavened bread" the Bible tells us (in Exodus 23:14 and elsewhere); seven days are observed in Israel today, as well as in the Diaspora by Reform and Reconstructionist Jews. Others celebrate for eight days, according to a Diaspora custom enacted into law by Hillel the Second, a fourth-century sage.

Jews in all places celebrate one festive meal. However, families in the Diaspora who observe the holiday for eight days hold two seders, one on each of the first two eves. Some special interest groups in synagogues or communities—such as gays and lesbians, women, the blind, or people whose families all came from the same place—now hold a third seder; these celebrations are held on the eve of the third day or, often, on a completely different evening, before or during Passover week.

Whether attending one, two, or three seders, each participant cannot help but feel a part of the large

Matzah Perforator Roller, Sweden, late 19th Century
The Israel Museum, Jerusalem

family of Jews across the world who are all celebrating a similar festive meal in the very same season. Each seder, the synthesis of thousands of years of change, still retains—and creates anew—the flavor and spirit of that first seder in biblical times. And, as an outgrowth of the exodus story, the seder continues to be a catalyst for social justice and ethical values.

The Bible dictates that Jews emphasize beauty during ritual observance: "This is my God and I will glorify (beautify) Him." (Exodus 15:2) Also, in the sixteenth century, Joseph Caro wrote, in the Code of Jewish Law (Shulhan Aruch), that the seder table is to be set "with beautiful vessels...in the manner of freedom." This has led to the creation of glorious illuminated illustrations and other stylized art in Passover haggadahs, and to a variety of magnificent ritual objects and fine textiles with which to observe the holiday. Ranging from treasured family heirlooms to fine museum pieces, such items attest to the skill and imagination of artists and artisans throughout history. Collectively, these works present the splendor of the holiday and the theme of freedom that Passover represents.

A note on usage and spelling:

In general, Ashkenazi(c) Jews, or Ashkenazim, are those Jews whose families came from Poland, Russia, Germany, and northern France. In general, Sephardi(c) Jews, or Sephardim, are those whose families came from Spain, and whose travels (after the expulsion in 1492) took them to places such as Holland, southern France, North Africa, Greece, Italy, and Turkey. Some people use the term Sephardic to refer to all Jews who are not Ashkenazic.

We have used both *ch* and *h* to reflect the guttural sound of the Hebrew letters *chaf* and *chet*, as in *hametz*, *Pesach*, and *baruch*. And we have chosen the Sephardic Hebrew pronunciation used in Israel for words such as *haroset*, and all the blessings. To form the plurals of the words matzah and haggadah, we have added *s*, to correspond to the pronunciation used by most American Jews.

A Family at the Seder, *First Cincinnati Haggadah* (Detail), Southern Germany, c. 1480
Klau Library, Hebrew Union College—Jewish Institute of Religion, Cincinnati

Order of the Seder

- Candle lighting (the lights of festivals)
- *Kiddush*—blessing over wine (the fruit of the vine)
- Drinking the first cup of wine
- Washing the hands
- *Karpas*—blessing over green vegetables (the fruit of the soil) and eating
- Breaking the middle matzah and hiding the *afikoman*
- Telling the story:

  "This is the bread of affliction…."

  The Four Questions

  The Exodus story—including The Four Sons, Bondage, The Ten Plagues, Leaving Egypt
- *Dayenu*—"It would have been enough!" or "How many wondrous deeds God has done for us!"
- Explanation of Symbols:

  Pesach (bone)

  Matzah (unleavened wafer)

  Maror (bitter herbs)
- Hallelujah—Praises to God (Readings from the Psalms)
- Drinking the second cup of wine
- Washing the hands—with a blessing
- Blessings over bread, matzah, and bitter herbs
- Making a Hillel sandwich:

  matzah

  bitter herbs

  haroset for every person to eat
- Dinner!
- Finding the *afikoman* and eating a piece
- Grace after meals
- Drinking the third cup of wine
- Welcoming Elijah
- Psalms and Prayers (*Hallel*)
- Drinking the fourth cup of wine
- "Next Year in Jerusalem" and Closing with Songs

קדש
אימפ׳יסא איל ביקירו
בין פ׳ינו די יינו
איר די קדש לאורי
אל סינ׳ור דיו׳נו:

ורחץ
לאורי לי מאנו קון
אוני׳ו מונד׳יצה
סינצה פ׳אר ברכה
קון פולוטיצה:

כרפס
גיל הרוסת׳ה דיל
אורי אינפ׳ונדרירא
ו׳רא פ׳רי
הבינד׳ורא:

יחץ
איל שמור
דין אי מיזו די
איסו סיאה סיד
אפ׳יקומן ריפושטו
אי מיסו:

מגיד
דירא׳י לה הגדה
קומי אי קי ס
שקרטו דא הא
מא סין קי איל
טו אביידיטו:

רחצה
לטרה וולטה
טי לי מאני
קון ורכה סינצה
פ׳נטירירי ואני:

הלל
נפוק קומינצ׳ה
אית איל הלל
פ׳ינישי אי ק׳יל
טי אה ס׳אלוטו
בונדיטי:

מוציא מצה
פ׳יליה איל שמור די
סופ׳ה אי צי פ׳ארי
המוציא לחם מן
מאניארי
מה כפ׳צה קולה מיר
אי דישו פוי׳ על
אכילה מצה מאני׳ה
אצפי דואין:

מרור
גיל הרוסת לטוקה
אוורא׳י אינפ׳וסה
קון דיר על אכילת
מרור קי ס אושה:

כורך
דיל טידצו שמור
וולני אין אונ׳רה
פ׳וליה אי דיזכר
למקדש דיבאלה
וולייה:

שלחן עורך
קונצ׳יה לה מיסה
אי איל צ׳בו אין
בוקה קאצ׳ה
אי מאני׳ה קואנטו
וא׳י קן פרו טי
פ׳אצ׳ה:

צפון
ל אפ׳יקומן קי נ׳ה
אירישרבאטו
אין פ׳ון קון דיוצ׳ין
ס׳ארר מאני׳אטו:

ברך
סינצה מאני׳אר נ׳
ביר אלטרו
פ׳וקורה דיר
ברכה אי פ׳ר
זמון פ׳ון קורה:

נרצה:
פ׳רונה אידיאו קי
איל בון וולייר
איצ׳טה אי קי אין
ירושלם צ׳ר רימטה
א ב״ב:

בה
זה השער לי׳ צדיקים
יבאו בו

סדר הגדה
של פסח

עם פרוש יפה ולשון אשכנז ועם ציורים מתפעונים נחים
מבאורתות וחידותם פענסה הקב׳ה לאבותינו במצרים
וצורת בית המקדש תוצב אכיר הלכתבתי׳ר מחס עלקלא
נחק ופרין יפה וגמתב כדפום

אמשטרדם

ונכתב פהקק פיורדא אצל נירנבורג לסדר
ולפרט אשרי אדם מצא חכמה והורע
דיך במדינת הקודש לפק

עירוב תבשילין

ברוך אתה יי אלהינו מלך העולם
אשר קדשנו במצותיו וצונו
על מצות ערוב
יהא שרא לנו לאפויי ולבשולי
ולאטמוני לאצלויי ולאדלוקי
שירגא ולמיעבד כל צרכנא מיומא טבא
לשבתא לנו ולכל ישראל

THE HAGGADAH: BOOK OF FREEDOM

EVERY PASSOVER SEDER FOCUSES on the telling of the exodus story, usually emphasizing God's role in liberating the children of Israel from the oppressive yoke of Pharaoh. Telling the biblical story, commenting on it in word and song, and following the many rituals that arose in connection with the story, required a unique book to establish the order of the many activities conducted at the seder table.

The haggadah is the book that serves as the guide or manual, to provide structure for the special festive meal; it is virtually the same in every Jewish home across the world, despite differences of background and language. Evolved over centuries, the haggadah is a compilation of passages from the Bible, Talmud, and Midrash, including commentaries, hymns, and songs of praise to God. In many families their haggadahs, stained from years of use, are handed down from one generation to another, and lovingly taken out each year for this seder meal.

The word "haggadah" comes from the Hebrew verb "to tell." The Torah commands: "And thou shalt tell thy son—on that day, saying: It is because of that which the Lord did for me when I came forth out of Egypt." (Exodus 13:8) And every year as the story is told, it gains new life, for each seder participant is instructed in the haggadah "to act as if he (she) was a slave in Egypt." Each person is encouraged to identify with those who suffer injustice in the contemporary world, and to strive to bring freedom to those in need of liberation. During or after times of extreme oppression, such as the expulsion of Jews from Spain, or the Holocaust, the haggadah included special prayers and illustrations that tied these oppressive events to the biblical plight of the Israelites.

The haggadah, as we know it today, has had a long journey. Although it appeared centuries before the common era (B.C.E.), by the second century C.E. the book took shape and corresponded to the home celebrations of the festive seder meal. The first full recording of what is considered the present-day haggadah was part of a ninth-century prayer book—although fragments from earlier books were found in Cairo at the turn of the nineteenth century. In southern and western Europe during the thirteenth through the

Haggadah, Germany, 1734
The Jewish Museum, New York

fifteenth centuries, the haggadah was separated from the prayer book—partly because the Bible and the Talmud forbade depiction of the human form, and so there were no illustrated prayer books. But these injunctions were relaxed for the haggadah. Perhaps because the book was meant to be used only at home, illustrating haggadahs became popular practice; consequently, beautiful hand-painted manuscripts and miniatures appeared. Some of these, commissioned by wealthy families, included the Golden and Rylands Haggadahs from Spain and the Darmstadt from Germany.

The invention of the printing press in the fifteenth century created an opportunity for broader distribution of these books. But printing techniques were relatively crude, and machine-printed haggadahs remained inferior to hand-printed manuscripts; where affordable, both types of haggadahs were used. As the number of books printed in Hebrew increased in Italy, Turkey, and other safe havens for post-expulsion Jews, haggadahs were often named for their city of production, and mirrored, in text and art, the wanderings of the Jewish people, the historical/political climates in which they lived, and the influences of surrounding religious cultures. The Mantua Haggadah (sixteenth-century Italy) displays characters copied from Michaelangelo's Sistine Chapel; in the same book, Abraham, who remained a central figure through eighteenth-century haggadahs (the

Patriarchs were a favorite subject), is depicted riding in a gondola on the Euphrates. In the same century in Venice, a major center of Jewish printing, haggadahs sprouted in Yiddish and Judeo-Spanish, to meet the needs of different refugee populations from Germany and Spain. By the nineteenth century there was a permanent Hebrew press, and haggadahs appeared all over the world. A haggadah from Poona, India, printed in Marathi (the local language) and Hebrew, shows women, dressed in saris, preparing matzahs.

By the end of the twentieth century over three thousand different haggadahs, usually in Hebrew and the vernacular, or in a Jewish language—such as Yiddish, Judeo-Persian, Judeo-Spanish (Ladino)—had been printed. These reflected twentieth-century concerns: immigration, the development of different Jewish religious movements, the Holocaust, the "ingathering of exiles" in Israel, the rise of Zionism and the kibbutz, the emergence of the military, and a rising interest in the concerns of women. During this past century, individual Jewish artists interested in Jewish themes gave visual expression to the text of the haggadah; the work of artists such as Arthur Szyk, Ben Shahn, Marc Chagall, and others rival the manuscripts of earlier centuries. Today, thanks to these artists and to the development of printing, each seder participant can have his or her own beautiful haggadah for the Passover celebration.

Eating the Green Vegetable/Drinking the Wine
Rylands Sephardic Haggadah, Catalonia, mid–late 14th Century
The John Rylands University Library of Manchester, England

The seder begins with the sanctification of the wine in a special blessing called the "*Kiddush*." Soon after that, a small piece of green vegetable (called "*karpas*") is blessed and eaten. Here, as in subsequent haggadahs, people are clad in contemporary dress.

שֵׁר לְבֵית אֲבֹת עֵה
לְבֵית

וְלָקְחוּ מִן הַדָּם וְנָתְנוּ
עַל שְׁתֵּי הַמְּזוּזֹת
צְלִי אֵשׁ

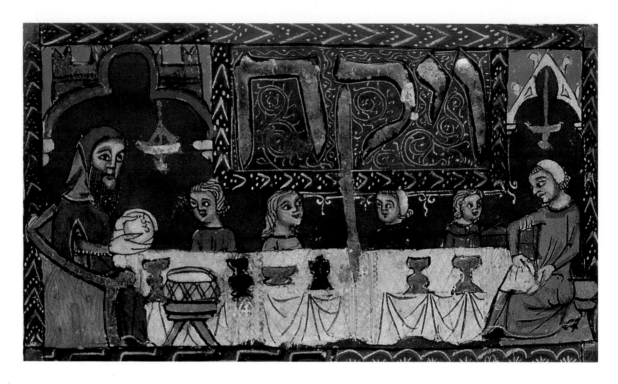

BREAKING THE MATZAH
BARCELONA HAGGADAH, c. 1350

The British Library, London

At the beginning of the seder, the leader
breaks the middle matzah in half and hides it.
This broken piece is called the "*afikoman*"
(from the Greek "dessert") because it is the
last food to be consumed at the seder.
The children search for the *afikoman* and
demand a ransom as a reward.

———

In parts of Morocco it was the custom to break the middle
matzah into the letter *hay*, one of the names of God.

HA LACHMA ANYA
THE HAGGADAH IN MEMORY
OF THE HOLOCAUST
UNITED STATES, 1981

Designed and illustrated by David Wander
Calligraphy by Yonah Weinrib
Courtesy of the Artist

The text for *Ha Lahma Anya* is graphically integrated with
a Jewish star on this dramatic Haggadah page:

*This is the bread of affliction which our ancestors ate in the
land of Egypt. Let all who are hungry come and eat.
Let all who are in need come and celebrate Passover.
This year we are here: Next year, in the land of Israel!
This year we are slaves: Next year may we be free!*

הָא לַחְמָא עַנְיָא דִּי
אֲכָלוּ אַבְהָתָנָא בְּאַרְעָא
דְמִצְרַיִם. כָּל דִכְפִין יֵיתֵי
וְיֵיכֹל. כָּל דִצְרִיךְ יֵיתֵי
וְיִפְסַח. הָשַׁתָּא הָכָא.
לְשָׁנָה הַבָּאָה בְּאַרְעָא
דְיִשְׂרָאֵל. הָשַׁתָּא עַבְדֵי.
לְשָׁנָה הַבָּאָה בְּנֵי
חוֹרִין.

**BUILDING PHARAOH'S CITIES
LEIPNIK HAGGADAH, HAMBURG/ALTONA
GERMANY, 1740**

Joseph ben David Leipnik

The British Library, London

OPPOSITE:
**THE FOUR QUESTIONS
THE HAGGADAH, LONDON, 1940**

Arthur Szyk

Library of Congress, Washington, D.C.

At the Passover seder, the youngest child asks
this question: "How is this night different from
all other nights?" The child then asks four
additional questions, the answers to which are
the telling of the exodus story. Although this
custom began in Europe in the seventeenth
century, in some places (such as parts of North
Africa) everyone asked the questions together,
or the father asked, and the children answered.

**"THEY MADE THEIR LIVES BITTER WITH HARD LABOR, IN MORTAR AND
IN BRICK, AND ALL MANNER OF HARD WORK IN THE FIELDS."** (EXODUS 1:14)

23

THE FOUR SONS
WASHINGTON HAGGADAH
NORTHERN ITALY OR
CENTRAL EUROPE, 1478

Joel Ben Simeon

Library of Congress, Washington, D.C.

The language of the Torah suggests four types of children to
whom the exodus story may be told: a wise son, a wicked
son, a simple son, and one too young to ask questions.
Here we see the wicked son dressed in the garb of a soldier.

"...AND THE LORD HEARD OUR VOICE, AND SAW OUR
AFFLICTION AND OUR LABOR AND OUR OPPRESSION..." (DEUTERONOMY 26:7)

LEAVING EGYPT
HISPANO-MORESQUE HAGGADAH
CASTILE, c. 1300

The British Library, London

"**AND MIRIAM SANG UNTO THEM: 'SING TO THE LORD, FOR HE HAS TRIUMPHED GLORIOUSLY.'**" (EXODUS 15:21)

**MIRIAM AND HER MAIDENS SING AND DANCE
GOLDEN HAGGADAH, BARCELONA, c. 1320**

The British Library, London

A special reading honoring Puah and Shifra is recited at some seders,
particularly in women's circles—they were the midwives who refused
to obey Pharaoh's decree to kill Hebrew babies. Yoheved, mother
of Moses, and Miriam, his sister who helped save him, are also
honored. The Talmud (Sotah) tells us that because of the labors of
the Hebrew women, all the children of Israel were liberated.

27

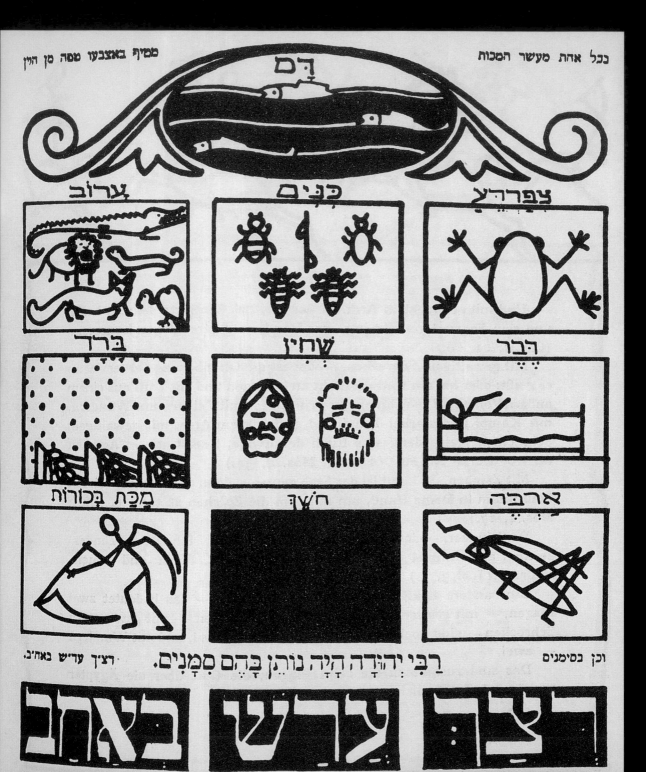

THE TEN PLAGUES
GEISMAR HAGGADAH, BERLIN, 1928

Otto Geismar

Library of Congress, Washington, D.C.

God inflicted ten plagues upon the people and the land of Egypt: blood, frogs, lice, wild beasts, cattle disease, boils, hail, locusts, darkness, death of the first born.

At the time of the haggadah reading, when each of the plagues is recited, it is customary for every participant to dip his/her pinky finger into a glass of wine, and to shake that bit of wine onto a small plate. Perhaps this is a reminder that the Egyptians who drowned in the Red Sea were also children of God; therefore, we should not be so proud as to drink with a full cup.

THE BITTER HERBS
HISPANO-MORESQUE HAGGADAH
CASTILE, c. 1300

The British Library, London

The eating of bitter herbs, prescribed in the Torah, was later interpreted by the rabbis. Seder participants identify this action with the bitterness endured by the children of Israel in bondage, and also with the bitter herbs eaten at the first seder, as commanded by God. During the seder a piece of bitter herbs (*maror*) is mixed with the symbolic *haroset* and eaten—after a proper blessing. Soon after that, each participant eats a tiny sandwich of matzah and a bit of *maror*, as did Hillel, a great sage of the first century B.C.E.

"IN EVERY GENERATION EACH PERSON MUST SEE HIM(HER)SELF AS IF HE(SHE) CAME OUT OF EGYPT."

(MISHNAH PESAHIM 10:5)

**IN EVERY GENERATION
HAGGADAH IN MEMORY OF THE HOLOCAUST
UNITED STATES, 1981**

Designed and illustrated by David Wander

Calligraphy by Yonah Weinrib

Courtesy of the Artist

These words from the haggadah, overshadowed by the
concentration-camp uniform, bind the recent Holocaust in
Europe with the enslavement of the Israelites long ago.

בְּכָל
דּוֹר
וָדוֹר

חַיָּב אָדָם
לִרְאוֹת אֶת
עַצְמוֹ כְּאִלּוּ
הוּא יָצָא
מִמִּצְרַיִם,
שֶׁנֶּאֱמַר:
וְהִגַּדְתָּ
לְבִנְךָ בַּיּוֹם
הַהוּא לֵאמֹר:
בַּעֲבוּר זֶה
עָשָׂה יְיָ

לִי, בְּצֵאתִי
מִמִּצְרָיִם. לֹא
אֶת אֲבוֹתֵינוּ
בִּלְבַד גָּאַל
הַקָּדוֹשׁ בָּרוּךְ
הוּא, אֶלָּא
אַף אוֹתָנוּ
גָּאַל עִמָּהֶם,
שֶׁנֶּאֱמַר:
וְאוֹתָנוּ הוֹצִיא
מִשָּׁם, לְמַעַן
הָבִיא אֹתָנוּ,
לָתֶת לָנוּ
אֶת הָאָרֶץ
אֲשֶׁר נִשְׁבַּע
לַאֲבוֹתֵינוּ.

> "**AT THIS MOMENT, THEN,
> WE THANK GOD:
> WE PRAISE, GLORIFY,
> EXALT AND BLESS THE
> POWER THAT DID ALL
> THESE MIRACLES FOR
> OUR ANCESTORS AND US.**"
>
> (THE PASSOVER HAGGADAH)

PRAISES TO GOD
DARMSTADT HAGGADAH
GERMANY, LATE 15TH CENTURY

Israel ben Meir of Heidelberg

Universitäts-und Landesbibliothek Darmstadt

At this point in the seder, participants are
instructed to lift the cup of wine and recite
the affirmation highlighted on this page.

ELIJAH
WASHINGTON HAGGADAH
NORTHERN ITALY OR CENTRAL EUROPE, 1478

Joel Ben Simeon

Library of Congress, Washington, D.C.

Elijah was a prophet in Israel who, according to the Bible
(2 Kings 2:11), did not die but rose to heaven. It is believed
that he will return to earth to announce the coming of
the Messiah. Then the Gate of Mercy in Jerusalem (presently
sealed) will open for him, ushering in a time of peace.

"PEACE BE WITHIN THY WALLS, AND PROSPERITY WITHIN THY PALACES."

(PSALMS 122:7)

NEXT YEAR IN JERUSALEM
SECOND CINCINNATI HAGGADAH
MORAVIA, c. 1716

Klau Library, Hebrew Union College—Jewish
Institute of Religion, Cincinnati

Images of the Holy Temple and the walls of ancient
Jerusalem are depicted in many haggadahs. At the
end of the seder Jews recite in unison, "Next year
in Jerusalem!" or, in Israel, "Next year in Jerusalem
rebuilt!" For thousands of years, Jerusalem has
been the holiest of all cities, to which Jews in the
Diaspora have longed to return. Another hope is
that this year in Jerusalem the Messiah will come,
ushering in a time of redemption and peace for all.

"WHO KNOWS FOUR?"

(PASSOVER SONG, "WHO KNOWS ONE?")

THE FOUR MATRIARCHS
THE NEW UNION HAGGADAH
UNITED STATES, 1982

Leonard Baskin

Courtesy of the Artist's Estate

Thus begins a verse from one of a group of songs that
closes the seder: "Who knows four?" The number four
represents the Matriarchs of the Jewish people—Sarah,
Rebecca, Leah, and Rachel.

SEDER PLATES

THE PASSOVER TABLE is traditionally set with beautiful objects—the family's finest silver, china, glassware, and linens. A lovely illustrated haggadah rests at each place setting, and a decorative and unique plate sits before the seder leader. This plate (called *ke'arah*) holds the special foods symbolic of the exodus story and the Passover celebration at the Holy Temple. Participants at the seder fulfill their obligations of religious law—both biblical and rabbinic—by eating or acknowledging these foods. Although the foods may vary somewhat from region to region, they are basically the same in every Jewish home:

An egg (*betzah*), roasted slightly or, as in North Africa, dyed with tea bags to look brown and burned, is a symbol of mourning for the Temple in Jerusalem. The egg also symbolizes spring and new life.

A slightly roasted lamb bone (*z'roa*)—or its substitute, a chicken neck—is a reminder of the Paschal sacrifice in the Holy Temple. Vegetarians may use a broiled beet instead, because it too bleeds like an animal.

Celery, lettuce, or parsley (*karpas*) is another sign of spring. The greens should be bunched, to reflect the hyssop plant that was used on the first seder night to splash the blood of the Paschal lamb on the doorposts of the Israelites.

A bitter food (*maror*)—generally horseradish root, but also artichokes (Gibraltar), romaine lettuce (Yemen), or potato peels in remembrance of the Holocaust—serves as a reminder of the bitterness of slavery. A sixth place on the plate may hold extra horseradish or romaine, called *hazeret*, for making a matzah sandwich as part of the seder ritual.

A mixture of chopped fruit and nuts (*haroset*) resembles mortar, and symbolizes the bricks that the children of Israel were forced to make for Pharaoh, during their bondage in Egypt.

A beautiful plate holding three matzahs also sits on the table to remind participants of the flat, unleavened wafers baked by the children of Israel in their rush to leave Egypt; according to biblical law, this is the only type of bread permitted during all the days of the festival. The plate can be flat and decorated, or draped with a beautiful cloth to cover the matzahs. Sometimes, as in eighteenth-century Europe and as is fashionable at the present time, the matzah plate is set under or attached to the seder plate.

Tiered Seder Plate, Vienna, 1814, Franz Strobl
SILVER: CAST, PIERCED, AND ENGRAVED
HUC Skirball Cultural Center, Museum Collection, Los Angeles

The three matzahs symbolize the three types of Jews: Cohens, a high priestly caste; Levites, another priestly class; and Israelites, who were the largest group. All three took part in the sacrifices at the Holy Temple.

Although the shapes, styles, and decorations of seder plates have continued to evolve for thousands of years, most had indentations or containers to hold the five special foods. The Mishnah, compiled in the first few centuries of the Common Era, mentions one plate to hold the symbolic seder foods, but it is unknown if these were decorated. Special plates or containers to hold matzahs also appear in illustrated haggadahs of the Middle Ages.

Both Jewish and non-Jewish skilled craftsmen used the same materials and techniques to satisfy the demand for seder plates. From fifteenth-century Spain, a ceramic seder plate features the designs and tin-glazed surface of Hispano-Moresque lusterware. From the sixteenth to the twentieth century, Jews living in the Middle East were excellent metalsmiths who created artistic designs in copper and other metals. Wealthy families living in Germany in the eighteenth and nineteenth centuries commissioned lavish and ornate silver plates, while the majority of European Jews bought plates made of pewter, an inexpensive alternative used for many domestic items.

The iconography adorning seder plates also varied with local customs and traditions. In the Middle East, for instance, decorative motifs were drawn from geometric forms and Arabic calligraphy, integrating Muslim designs with Jewish prayers. In Christian Europe during the Middle Ages, biblical scenes echoing famous Christian paintings, manuscripts, and miniatures appeared on plates used for the holiday.

But, in order to "make Jewish" or Judaize these plates, and to reinforce the many messages of the seder—the greatness of God, the miracle of the exodus, the importance of freedom—Jewish craftsmen often embellished their seder plates with the Jewish star, scenes from the seder meal, the exodus story, illustrations from haggadahs, and more. Hebrew writing—that is, the Holy Tongue—was added as early as the fifteenth century, and continues to decorate contemporary plates. Thus, the phrases noting the order of the seder, the Passover blessings, and the names of the seder foods transform an ordinary object into an artistic and sacred Jewish ceremonial piece.

"THE TORAH SPEAKS OF FOUR TYPES OF CHILDREN: ONE WISE, ONE WICKED, ONE SIMPLE, AND ONE TOO YOUNG TO ASK QUESTIONS."

(THE PASSOVER HAGGADAH)

GERMANY, 1790

PEWTER: ENGRAVED

Hechal Shlomo, The Sir Isaac and Lady Edith
Wolfson Museum of Jewish Art, Jerusalem

The rim of this pewter plate states the order of
the seder; the inner part portrays the sacrificial
lamb and the Four Sons, both part of the story
told in the haggadah. Pewter, less expensive than
silver and easily engraved and polished, was used
to make domestic objects for the masses.

"...GO THEREFORE AND WORK,...DELIVER YOUR QUOTA OF BRICKS."

(EXODUS 5:18)

VIENNA, c. 1870

SILVER: CAST, REPOUSSÉ, ENGRAVED, AND GILT

The Israel Museum, Jerusalem

On this ornate plate, a pair of lions flanks the Ten
Commandments under the Crown of the Torah—an
icon found on Torah curtains, Hanukkah lamps, and
other Jewish ceremonial objects. Five separate vessels—
each in a different shape—hold the symbolic foods.
These include a small wheelbarrow—for *haroset*—that
reminds us of the cement (mortar) carried by the
Israelites when they were slaves in Egypt.

HUNGARY, 19ᵀᴴ CENTURY

EARTHENWARE: GLAZED

Hechal Shlomo, The Sir Isaac and Lady Edith Wolfson
Museum of Jewish Art, Jerusalem

A family at the seder table is pictured on this plate. They
are surrounded by the Aramaic words, "*Ha lahma anya*—
This is the bread of affliction," the blessing over the
greens (*karpas*), and the *shehecheyanu* blessing, recited
upon reaching a new season or holiday.

46

JERUSALEM, 19TH CENTURY

EARTHENWARE: GLAZED

Hechal Shlomo, The Sir Isaac and Lady Edith Wolfson
Museum of Jewish Art, Jerusalem

In Jewish tradition, grapes (and wine) are symbols
of joy. Fittingly, vines, leaves, and clusters of
grapes dominate this Passover plate. According
to the Mishnah, grapes were permitted as first
offerings at the Temple in Jerusalem.

"THY KINGDOM IS ENDURING AND THY DOMINION ENDURETH THROUGHOUT ALL GENERATIONS." (PSALMS 145:13)

ISRAEL, 1889

WOOD: CARVED AND PAINTED

The Israel Museum, Jerusalem

This unique wooden plate
features a relief of the Western Wall in
Jerusalem that symbolizes the hope of
redemption and the rebuilding of the Temple.
The Hebrew lettering is part of a prayer
sung in the synagogue on Sabbath before
the removal of the Torah from the
Ark (and subsequent reading).

POLAND, 19ᵀᴴ CENTURY

CERAMIC: FAIENCE

Haaretz Museum, Tel Aviv

A tool for perforating matzah accompanies this
earthenware plate, on which is written "*Hag Hamatzot*"
or "Festival of Matzahs," one of the names of the holiday.
Ceramics for Passover were a specialty in Potylicz,
the town in Poland where this plate was made.

"**AND THE CHILDREN OF THE CAPTIVITY...KEPT THE FEAST OF UNLEAVENED BREAD SEVEN DAYS WITH JOY; FOR THE LORD HAD MADE THEM JOYFUL.**" (EZRA 6:19-22)

VIENNA, c. 1900

CERAMIC: GLAZED PORCELAIN

Maker: LQR

The Jewish Museum, New York

During the eighteenth to the early-twentieth century, a large Jewish population resided in Vienna. The city became a center for the *Haskalah* movement that encouraged secularization, assimilation in language, and eventual emancipation. Vienna also became a hub of Zionist activity in the twentieth century, because an influx of Zionist Jews from Eastern Europe had settled there. The Star of David identifies this plate as a Jewish object.

PERSIA, 20ᵀᴴ CENTURY

COPPER

Musée du Judaisme, Paris/Réunion des Musées Nationaux

In addition to the matzahs and the names of the seder
foods, this beautiful plate celebrates the wine at the
seder; here we see a cup of wine and decanters labeled
"old wine," plus the surrounding *Kiddush* and praise
to God for having brought us to this season.

BAGHDAD, 20ᵀᴴ CENTURY

GOLD, SILVER, AND BRONZE SET IN COPPER

Hechal Shlomo, The Sir Isaac and Lady Edith Wolfson Museum
of Jewish Art, Jerusalem

Symbols of the twelve tribes and the exodus from
Egypt appear on this copper plate, embellished with
gold, silver, and bronze. Explanations for both are
given in beautiful Hebrew and Arabic script.

"You have seen...how I bore you on eagles' wings and brought you to Me." (Exodus 19:4)

AUSTRO-HUNGARY
c. EARLY 20ᵗʰ CENTURY

SILVER CAST

Spertus Museum/Spertus Institute of Jewish Studies, Chicago

Elaborate decorations include four eagles, appearing on
the edges of this plate. An imperial symbol of the
Hapsburgs, the eagle is also meaningful at Passover
because of its reference in the Bible. After the exodus—
during the desert wanderings of the Jewish people—
God told Moses to remind the Israelites of these wings,
and gave them the Ten Commandments.

FRANKFURT-AM-MAIN
GERMANY, 1930

Ludwig Wolpert

SILVER, EBONY, AND GLASS

The Jewish Museum, New York

This streamlined plate was created by a pioneer of the decorative arts and Jewish ritual objects. The spare style was influenced by the Bauhaus School of twentieth-century Germany, whose principles demanded that the design of an object echo its use. This unique plate combines, in one form, the seder plate, matzah holder, and the Cup of Elijah.

"ONE OF THE SUBTLEST OF THE ARTS IS THE ART OF MAKING

MEN LIVE TOGETHER IN PEACE." (FELIX FRANKFURTER, *THE PUBLIC AND ITS GOVERNMENT*)

SEDER PLATE AND **THE CUP OF WORLD PEACE**
(SEDER CUP), UNITED STATES, 1994
Tom Otterness
SILVER AND GOLD VERMEIL
The Jewish Museum, New York

> "**THEREFORE THEY DID SET OVER THEM TASKMASTERS TO AFFLICT THEM WITH THEIR BURDENS. AND THEY BUILT FOR PHARAOH STORE-CITIES, PITHOM AND RAAMSES.**"

(EXODUS 1:11)

GENERATION AFTER GENERATION WE KEEP OVERTURNING THE PYRAMIDS
UNITED STATES, 1996

Chava Wolpert Richard

CORIAN

Courtesy of the Artist

On this plate made by a contemporary artist, containers for the ceremonial foods are shaped like pyramids, to represent those built by the Israelites in Egypt. At the seder they are overturned, symbolizing the end of the oppressive Egyptian rule.

CUPS

AT THE BEGINNING OF EVERY SEDER, the leader recites a blessing over the wine, and then each person drinks one cup. The commandment to recite this blessing, or *Kiddush*—from the Hebrew word for sanctification—can be traced to the Babylonian Talmud (Pesahim 106a), completed in 500 C. E. During the seder three more cups are drunk—one before the meal and two after; in the Jerusalem Talmud (Pesahim 10:1)—completed approximately one hundred years before the Babylonian Talmud—these four cups are explained to represent the four ways that God will redeem the people: "I will free you from the slavery of Egypt. I will deliver you from their slavery. I will redeem you with an outstretched arm. I will take you to be my people." (Exodus 6) A fifth cup, added by some families, is said to represent another of God's promises: "I will bring you into the Land," and may now suggest thankfulness for the State of Israel.

All of these obligations, plus the offering of wine to Elijah the Prophet toward the end of the seder, created a need for special Passover cups, goblets, and beakers. For at least the past four hundred years, such vessels—made of glass, ivory, silver, gold, and other metals—have adorned the seder tables of Jews all over the world. Precious metals and fine glass were commissioned by the wealthy; base metals and less expensive glass, by the masses.

In biblical times, and as mentioned later in the Talmud, the sands of the Mediterranean shore were excellent for the making of glass; sand contains silica, which, when fused with other materials at high temperatures, creates the lustrous, translucent substance. According to some scholars, the tradition of glassmaking in the Middle East started in about the third millennium B.C.E. One theory is that the Amorites—a Semitic Mesopotamian tribe—moved to

Morocco, end of the 19th Century
SILVER
Hechal Shlomo, The Sir Isaac and Lady Edith Wolfson Museum of Jewish Art, Jerusalem

the Mediterranean coast and brought along the knowledge of glassmaking, which was then practiced by the Jews. Other scholars believe that glass originated in Egypt. It is known that Jews living in Judea in ancient times sent prized glass beads to the Far East in exchange for precious silk. Glass was a highly prized commodity in Northern Europe as well; the process was brought by Jews to the area along the Rhine in Roman times (first century C.E.), when glassmaking reached a high level of quality; for over a thousand years—during the Roman, Byzantine, and early Christian eras, and including the reign of the Crusaders in the Holy Land—Jewish craftsmen were accomplished glassmakers. And, in Germany hundreds of years later, the making of Jewish ceremonial glass was developed even further, with delicate acid etching.

Also, according to the beliefs of some scholars, Jews, for over a thousand years, were engaged in the smithing of metal; documents discovered in Cairo, at the turn of the nineteenth century, revealed that Jewish smiths practiced their trade in the Arab lands of North Africa and the Middle East since the early days of Islam. In the centuries that followed, because such work was considered too demeaning for Muslims, Jews crafted tools as well as vessels and ornaments, of silver, gold, brass, and copper. And despite being banned from working in Medieval craft guilds in Europe, Jews later fashioned beautifully decorated objects—firearms in seventeenth-century Poland, and silver cups in the same century and later in Eastern Europe, Germany, and Austria. By adding Hebrew words such as "Cup of Elijah" and also prayers and blessings, some of these beautiful non-ceremonial items became sacred cups for the Passover table.

Since the eighteenth century, in Ashkenazi and in many Sephardi homes, a large and beautifully crafted goblet called the Cup of Elijah has been filled with wine and set on the table. (Sometimes the cup is set atop the seder plate.) According to legend, Elijah the Prophet—herald of the Messiah—invisibly visits every Jewish home on Passover eve. Usually after the meal, the door is opened for the Prophet to enter, and the guests rise to greet him with a song of welcome.

In the 1980's a women's group in Boston felt that a special "Miriam's Cup" should be added to the Passover celebration, because Miriam the Prophetess played such an important role in the Passover story. According to the Torah, the sister of Moses (later identified as Miriam) watched from a distance as her infant brother was placed in a basket and set among the reeds of the river; she then suggested to the Egyptian princess who found the basket that her own mother be brought forth to nurse the child. And, according to the Book of Exodus, Miriam eventually led the women to freedom.

Bulgaria, 1698
SILVER
Hechal Shlomo, The Sir Isaac and Lady Edith Wolfson Museum of Jewish Art, Jerusalem
This cup—for the blessing over wine—might have also been used for the *Kiddush* at Passover.

"REMEMBER THIS DAY,
IN WHICH YOU CAME
OUT OF THE HOUSE
OF BONDAGE."

(EXODUS 13:3)

**NETHERLANDS
MID 18TH CENTURY**

Judaica Collection Max Berger, Vienna

This exquisite glass goblet portrays a
family at the Passover seder.

GERMANY, 18ᵀᴴ CENTURY

IVORY

Hechal Shlomo, The Sir Isaac and Lady Edith
Wolfson Museum of Jewish Art, Jerusalem

Ivory was a prized treasure even in biblical
times. King Solomon had the coveted material
brought from the upper Euphrates—then home
to the Syrian elephant—to Jerusalem, where it
was fashioned into "a great throne...and
overlaid...with the finest gold." (I Kings 10:18)

The carving on this magnificent cup
portrays Moses and Aaron at Pharaoh's court,
beseeching him to let the Israelites go free.
The name of the carver is also shown.

"AND THIS DAY SHALL BE A MEMORIAL AND YE SHALL KEEP IT A FEAST BY AN ORDINANCE FOREVER."

(EXODUS 12:14)

AUGSBURG, GERMANY, 1806

SILVER: REPOUSSÉ, CHASED, AND CAST

Spertus Museum/Spertus Institute of Jewish Studies, Chicago

The Hebrew words "Remember and Keep" on
this beautiful silver cup refer to the
biblical passage from Exodus.

"QUICKLY IN OUR DAYS MAY HE COME TO US, SON OF THE FAMILY OF DAVID."

(TRADITIONAL SONG TO WELCOME ELIJAH THE PROPHET)

MOSCOW, 1837
GU-GAVRILA UNSTINOV

PRECIOUS METALS: SILVER, NIELLO, ENGRAVED AND GILDED

The Gross Family Collection, Tel Aviv

This splendid cup was inscribed and presented as a gift to a learned Hasidic rebbe—the Rabbi Rav Yitzhak of Bender—by one of his disciples. The words "Cup of Elijah" were added later, transforming the cup into a sacred object for the Passover seder. According to tradition, the Messiah, heralded by Elijah, will be a descendant of the House of David.

In certain Hasidic circles, an empty cup is passed around, and everyone pours some wine into it while singing the song of welcome to Elijah. This shows that, symbolically, everyone can contribute to bettering the world.

68

BOHEMIA, 19TH CENTURY

GLASS: FREE-BLOWN, TOOLED, RUBY-FLASHED,
AND WHEEL ENGRAVED

The Jewish Museum, New York

Fine glassware of nineteenth-century
Bohemia displayed engraved
decorations and acid etchings, such
as those on the cup pictured here.

POSSIBLY GERMANY, MID 19ᵀᴴ CENTURY

SILVER. CAST AND ENGRAVED
The Israel Museum, Jerusalem

The leaves of the grape vine on this elegant cup symbolize wine consumed during the seder, and also represent one of the seven species of the land of Israel that God promised the Israelites. (Deuteronomy: 8) The Hebrew inscriptions—"How is this night different from all other nights?" and "Slaves we were in Egypt"—are from the text of the Haggadah.

71

"... WE SHALL LIVE AT LAST AS FREE MEN AND WOMEN ON OUR OWN SOIL." (THEODOR HERZL)

ISRAEL, 19TH CENTURY

BITUMEN STONE: TURNED AND CARVED

The Israel Museum, Jerusalem

The writing on this cup identifies it as a Cup of Elijah.
In addition, the cup displays the Western Wall—the only
remaining wall of the Holy Temple in Jerusalem—
Judaism's holiest site. In the Torah God also promises:
"I will bring you into the Land." This has led,
in some families, to the drinking of a fifth cup
of wine, in gratitude for the establishment
of the State of Israel, where all Jews may be free.

UKRAINE, c. 1910

Baruch Dornfeld

SILVER

Judaica Collection Max Berger, Vienna

Accompanied by the words "Remember the Exodus...," the intricate relief on this Art Nouveau cup shows the Israelites leaving Egypt.

UNITED STATES, 1997

Amy Klein Reichert

SILVER: CAST AND HAMMERED

The Jewish Museum, New York

These cups artistically represent Miriam's Well, which (according to Midrash) accompanied the Israelites throughout their desert wanderings. Whenever Israel made camp, the well followed and rested nearby. The water—said to have healing powers—flowed in all directions, nourishing all kinds of herbs, seeds, and trees. After Miriam died, the well stopped producing water. Although its whereabouts are unknown, it is believed to be somewhere in Israel, possibly in the Sea of Tiberias.

Miriam's cups are often blue—like the water of the well—and are adorned with bells and shells to suggest the sounds of her tambourine; they are filled with water, wine, flower petals, or sweet-smelling spices, which Miriam's Well was said to contain.

UNITED STATES, 20ᵗʰ CENTURY

Melanie Kline

STERLING SILVER, PEARLS

Courtesy of Melanie Kline

TEXTILES

THE RITUALS OF THE FESTIVAL—most dating from Mishnaic and Talmudic times—inspired special textiles for the festive seder meal. For at least the last four hundred years, unique towels for the washing of hands, beautiful covers for pillows on which the leader and other participants could lean, special bags for holding the three matzahs or the broken piece called the *afikoman*, ornate cloths for covering the matzahs, and decorative tablecloths have contributed to the beauty of the seder table.

Sometimes these textiles were created for general use and later tailored specifically for Passover rituals. As with metalwork and glass, regional customs and motifs influenced the designs and iconography that appeared on these seder textiles: in nineteenth-century Alsace, where embroidery and painting were established folk arts, beautiful towels were displayed (by the general population) to cover other soiled towels used for hand washing. Jews adapted this custom for Passover by creating towels decorated with local flowers and the addition of Jewish symbols—the Garden of Eden, the Lions of Judah, and Passover blessings in Hebrew—in order to conceal towels actually used for the seder's ritual washing of hands. Colorful seder cloths from twentieth-century Iran appear embroidered with local floral and bird motifs, or in block-print designs typical of earlier Persian decorations. Passover blessings or passages from the haggadah differentiated these textiles from those of the general population and infused them with a holy intention.

The making of textiles is an important part of Jewish history. In biblical times fine linen and wool were woven, and natural silk was brought from the East for royalty and the very wealthy. Eventually, Jews in fourth-century C.E. Babylonia learned the art of raising silkworms to make silk for weaving, and developed their own industry (as alluded to in the Talmud). Sometime after the development of Islam (circa eighth century C.E.), Jews brought silk to Muslim

Passover Cover, Chalcis, Greece, Late 18th—early 19th Century
LINEN AND SILK
The Jewish Museum, New York

Spain; after their fifteenth-century expulsion from that land, itinerant merchants spread the knowledge of the silk and dyeing industry (in which Jews had a monopoly) to Turkey, parts of Italy, and other lands where Jews settled. Upper-class Europeans also valued this Mediterranean silk, and formed another market for Jewish goods. The weaving, dyeing, and merchandising of textiles continued to be in Jewish hands in Europe, Asia, and North Africa for centuries.

Jews also excelled in the adornment of textiles—painting beautiful scenes on fabric or embroidering delicate and intricate patterns. The designs varied, depending on the political and economic situation of the maker, as well as the techniques and cultural decoration of surrounding regions. Jews expelled from Spain, for example, brought the craft of embroidering gold thread (melted down from jewelry and coins) on silk velvet to North Africa, Italy, and southern Germany. In seventeenth-century Germany a special pillow case, or *laantuch*, was embroidered for the special seder pillow on which one leans; some scholars believe that the name "*laantuch*" comes from "*sich lehnen*," German for "to lean." And a few centuries later, Jews of northern, eastern, and western Europe continued to embroider on silk, linen, and cotton. Such decorations were made either by professionals—both men and women—or by girls and women only, who continued to form charming designs in folkloric traditions. In many places the textile included the name or initials of the needle worker, the person who commissioned it, or the person to whom it was given.

Jews excelled as well in the craft of weaving, a high art developed in Iran, Kurdistan, and other Muslim lands. Their brightly colored Passover rugs were either hung on the wall or put on the floor, where the seder participants sat while conducting their seder at low tables.

Passover Table Cover, Iran, 1921
COTTON: PRINTED WITH COLORED INK
The Gross Family Collection, Tel Aviv

The handheld matzah, an image known at least three centuries earlier in Italy, is featured on this Passover cloth. The word "Zion" inside the Star of David indicates the longing of Persian Jews for the land of Israel. Extensive inscriptions include the order of the seder and the foods on the seder plate.

In the Caucasus Mountains Jews were isolated and often found it difficult to get fresh foods for the Passover table. They would embroider the tablecloth with the symbols on the seder plate; thus they were assured of "fresh" seder foods each year.

"THE LORD LOVETH THE GATES OF ZION..." (PSALMS 87:2)

PILLOWCASE FOR PASSOVER SEDER
GERMANY, 18TH CENTURY

EMBROIDERED LINEN
HUC Skirball Cultural Center, Museum Collection, Los Angeles

This cover was made for the pillow on which the leader
of the seder leaned, and displays local flowers—
a favorite motif of embroiderers. These are intertwined
with Jewish symbols, such as rampant lions
(found on many Torah covers or Ark curtains), and the
spies sent by Joshua to survey the Promised Land.

"AND ALL THE GOODLINESS THEREOF IS AS THE FLOWER OF THE FIELD."

(ISAIAH 40:6)

AFIKOMAN BAG
CHINA, 19TH CENTURY

COTTON AND SATIN: EMBROIDERED
WITH SILK AND METALLIC THREAD

HUC Skirball Cultural Center, Museum Collection, Los Angeles

At the end of the meal the *afikoman*—the piece of
matzah broken and placed in the pouch at the start of
the seder—is found by the children and ransomed by
them for a small gift. Then, as a symbol of redemption
and reunion, it is brought together with the other
broken piece before the seder may resume. Each person
is obliged to eat a part of it, even though the portion is
allowed to be only the size of an olive, and no other
food may be eaten for the rest of the seder.

A modern interpretation might be, "How can
I make broken pieces whole in my own life?
In my family? My community?"

82

CEREMONIAL TOWEL FOR SEDER
WESTERN ASHKENAZIC, c. 1800

UNDYED LINEN EMBROIDERED WITH
RED COTTON AND POLYCHROME SILK

The Jewish Museum, New York

Such seder towels were used twice during
the seder, after the ritual washing of hands.
In Alsace, where half of France's Jews
lived at the beginning of the nineteenth
century, the art of needlework was well
developed and was passed down by women
from generation to generation.

PASSOVER TOWEL
POSSIBLY ALSACE, 1829

LINEN: PAINTED, OPEN WEAVE,
KNOTTED COTTON FRINGE

The Jewish Museum, New York

The Garden of Eden is painted with
watercolors on this fringed linen towel.

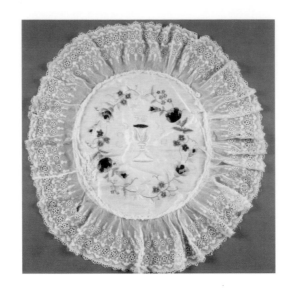

**MATZAH BAG
BIALYSTOCK, C. 1860**

The Jewish Museum, New York

Delicate lace and flowers surround a
Passover cup and inscription.

"...KNOW THAT TREES AND PLANTS AND FLOWERS HAVE LANGUAGE,
FEELING, AND PRAYER OF THEIR OWN." (ISRAEL BEN ELIEZER, THE BAAL SHEM TOV)

**MATZAH BAG
GERMANY, 19TH CENTURY**

UNDYED SILK/COTTON SATIN
EMBROIDERED WITH POLYCHROME SILK

The Jewish Museum, New York

The silk embroidery on this matzah bag
combines birds and delicate flowers—
often made from patterns—with
the "Festival of Matzahs" and the
embroiderer's initials in Hebrew.

MATZAH CASE
HUNGARY, 19ᵀᴴ CENTURY

VELVET: EMBROIDERED WITH FISH SCALES AND GOLD THREAD

Hechal Shlomo, The Sir Isaac and Lady Edith Wolfson Museum of Jewish Art, Jerusalem

For centuries matzah bags were fabricated in round shapes to accommodate the round,
handmade matzahs. The words on this lavish bag, embroidered with fish scales
and gold thread, celebrate the festival of unleavened bread. In Talmudic times
(the first few hundred years of the Common Era) matzahs had similar designs—birds,
fish, even chains of bondage. Later, the rabbis decided that these designs took
too much time to make (matzahs must be formed and baked within eighteen
minutes so as not to rise). Eventually, matzahs were simply perforated in rows.

MATZAH COVER
POLAND, 1894

Adela Schreiber

VELVET: EMBROIDERED WITH BRAID TRIM

HUC Skirball Cultural Center, Museum Collection, Los Angeles

This lovely matzah cover is embroidered with the closing words of the seder: "Next year in Jerusalem." The three tabs indicate the separation of the matzahs according to the three castes of Jews: Cohens, Levites, and Israelites.

"NEXT YEAR IN JERUSALEM." (THE PASSOVER HAGGADAH)

"SEVEN DAYS THOU SHALT EAT UNLEAVENED BREAD." (EXODUS 12:15)

MATZAH COVER
GERMANY, 1908

WOOL PETIT POINT ON CANVAS,
WITH SILK EMBROIDERY AND BRAID TRIM

HUC Skirball Cultural Center, Museum Collection, Los Angeles

With the invention of machinery to mass-produce
matzah, the shape of matzah changed from round to
square. On this cover the blessing over the matzah and
the biblical injunction are embroidered.

B'KOL DOR L'DOR (IN EVERY GENERATION)
MATZAH COVER, UNITED STATES, 2001

Jan Rabinowitch

LINEN WITH APPLIQUÉ

Oregon Jewish Museum

For thousands of years matzahs have been made at home, in community
ovens, and in special bakeries set up for that purpose. This stylized
contemporary matzah cover offers two passages from the haggadah:
"*Ha Lahma Anya*—This is the bread of affliction..." and "In every generation..."

BLESSINGS FOR THE SEDER

BASIC BEGINNING OF EVERY BLESSING:

Praised are You, Adonai our God, Sovereign of the Universe:

Baruch Atah Adonai Elohaynu Melech ha'olam

בָּרוּךְ אַתָּה יְיָ אֱלֹהֵינוּ מֶלֶךְ הָעוֹלָם:

(ADD ACCORDINGLY)

Who creates the fruit of the soil (karpas)

Boray p'ri ha'adamah

בּוֹרֵא פְּרִי הָאֲדָמָה

Who creates the fruit of the vine (wine)

Boray p'ri ha'gafen

בּוֹרֵא פְּרִי הַגָּפֶן

Who brings forth bread from the earth (bread)

Ha'motzi lechem min ha'aretz

הַמּוֹצִיא לֶחֶם מִן הָאָרֶץ

92

Who has kept us in life, sustained us, and brought us to this season (first night only)

She-he-che-yanu v'kiy'manu v'higi'anu lazman hazeh

שֶׁהֶחֱיָנוּ וְקִיְּמָנוּ וְהִגִּיעָנוּ לַזְּמַן הַזֶּה

Who has led us to holiness through His commandments, and commanded us:

Asher kid'shanu b'mitzvotav v'tzivanu

אֲשֶׁר קִדְּשָׁנוּ בְּמִצְוֹתָיו וְצִוָּנוּ:

to eat maror (bitter herbs)

al achilat maror

עַל אֲכִילַת מָרוֹר

to eat matzah (matzah)

al achilat matzah

עַל אֲכִילַת מַצָּה

to wash hands (washing hands before eating food)

al n'tilat yada-yim

עַל נְטִילַת יָדַיִם

to kindle the lights of festivals (candle lighting)

l'hadlik nayr shel yom tov

לְהַדְלִיק נֵר שֶׁל יוֹם טוֹב

MIGHTY IS HE—*ADIR HU*

This song, about seven hundred years old, was first sung in Germany. Each line begins with a different letter of the Hebrew alphabet.

FIRST VERSE:

Mighty is He. May God build the Temple soon.
Quickly, quickly. In our days, soon.

WHO KNOWS ONE? *EHAD, MI YODEA?*

This song has thirteen verses; each adds a number that has a link to Judaism.

LAST STANZA:

Thirteen are the attributes of God; Twelve, the tribes of Israel; Eleven, the stars in Joseph's dream; Ten, the Commandments; Nine, the months until childbirth; Eight, the days before the B'rit; Seven, the days of the week; Six, the orders of the Mishnah; Five, the books of Moses; Four, the Matriarchs; Three, the Patriarchs; Two, the tablets of the Law; One is almighty God, in heaven and on earth.

ONE LITTLE KID *HAD GADYA*

The cumulative verses of **Had Gadya,** sung for five hundred years in many different melodies, is an allegory about Jewish history: different characters represent Israel's oppressors: Babylon, Persia, Greece, Rome, etc. Strongest of all is the Holy One, who will bring peace to Israel.

LAST STANZA:

Along came the Holy One, blessed be He, and slaughtered the Angel of Death that killed the butcher who slew the ox that drank the water that quenched the fire that burned the stick that beat the dog that bit the cat that ate the kid that father bought for two zuzim. **Had Gadya. Had Gadya.**

"AND THE LORD BROUGHT US FORTH OUT OF EGYPT, WITH A MIGHTY HAND AND WITH AN OUTSTRETCHED ARM...."

(DEUTERONOMY 26:8)

To Professor Dov Noy, my friend and teacher, who instilled in me a love of the Jewish folk, and a passion for their lore.

ACKNOWLEDGMENTS

A note of special thanks to Anne Kostick at Stewart, Tabori & Chang, who first had the vision of this book. Special thanks also to Susan Wechsler, my editor at Fair Street Productions, and to Don Rush, companion in all my endeavors, both of whose wisdom, humor, and encouragement accompanied me on this book's entire journey. I am grateful also to Jon Glick, the designer who made this book so beautiful, and to Shaie Dively at Photosearch, Inc., who tracked down all the artwork.

I am indebted to the following people who helped locate and explain material: Rachel Ariel, Nurit Bank, Dr. Marc Bregman, Joan Cohen, Rabbi John Friedman, Dr. Haya Gavish, Fred and Ingrid Hertz, Hy Marks, Gisela Romang de Baler, Cherie Karo Schwartz, Simcha Shemesh, and David Winer.

I would like to acknowledge the following writers and editors whose works were essential to this research project: Penina V. Adelman, E. M. Broner, Louis Ginsberg, Philip Goodman, Joseph Gutmann, Lionel Kochan, Samuel Kurinsky, Vivian B. Mann, Bezalel Narkiss, Rabbi Stephan O. Parnes, Chaim Raphael, Cherie Karo Schwartz, Yosef Hayim Yerushalmi, Rabbi David Zaslow: to Encyclopedia Judaica, and to publications of the Israel Museum, Jerusalem; the Jewish Museum, New York; the Wolfson Museum, Jerusalem; and the Florida Holocaust Museum. And, finally, my sincere thanks to the museums and collections from which these beautiful works were selected.

Sources consulted included prayer books of the Conservative, Jewish Renewal, Orthodox, Reconstructionist, and Reform movements. Bible excerpts are reprinted primarily from the *The Holy Scriptures According to the Masoretic Text. A New Translation* ©1952, JPS.